Divine Dividends

Divine Dividends

by

Grace Diane Jessen

Illustrated by Lucille R. Perry

HORIZON PUBLISHERS

3rd Printing

INTERNATIONAL STANDARD BOOK NUMBER
0-88290-010-2

Printed in the
United States of America
by

HORIZON
PUBLISHERS
Post Office Box 490
55 East 300 South
Bountiful, Utah 84010
292-1959

4

Contents

A companion volume, **Royal Rewards,** has been prepared by the author. Its poetry conveys a tribute to fatherhood suitable for Father's Day, birthdays, or any occasion where "I love you" is appropriate. Also available from **Horizon Publishers.**

Divine Dividends

When a mother starts counting her fortune
   And figures her profit and loss,
She considers the matters financial
   To be unimportant and dross.

In the balance, the things that she values
   More highly than money or wealth
Are the love of her noble, good husband,
   The home that they share, and their health.

She has blessings that she cannot measure,
   Her faith, and her family and friends,
And the joys she receives through her children
   Are simply divine dividends.

Thoughts While Waiting

As I feel the gentle stirring
Of the new life here within me,
How I marvel at my fortune:
Never came a greater blessing
Than this miracle of Heaven!
And I wonder as I'm waiting
What the Lord will choose to send me.

Will it be a little daughter
Born with curls of sunny softness?
Will her cheeks be pink as rosebuds
And her tender skin like satin?
Will I fashion with my needle
Ruffled gowns of white and yellow
For a dainty maid to grow in?

Or perhaps in God's great wisdom
Will He send a son to bless us?
Will it be a son with bright eyes,
Blue and clear as deep lake water,
Born with legs both long and sturdy,
Blessed with music in his fingers
And with dimples like his father?

If a son or if a daughter
Shall be sent—it will not matter;
Each would find a loving welcome.
But a solemn thought disturbs me:
Can I meet the duty's challenge
To be wise and understanding
When I am at last a mother?

New Witness

My baby breathed earth's air today
And laid his cheek against my breast;
With tiny fingers clutching mine
He drifted into peaceful rest.

But sleeping there within my arm
The message that he brought was clear:
There is a God who reigns supreme,
Who made us all and sent us here.

Mementos of Motherhood

Every mother has a storehouse
    in a corner of her heart
That is filled with treasured keepsakes
    of her life, the priceless part,
And she sometimes likes to polish
    all these gems of truth and good
And recall her highly cherished
    mementos of motherhood.

A Baby is a Springtime Blossom

A baby is a springtime blossom
Pink and white on fragile green
Uniquely delicate and yet
Quite similar to every other
Baby you have ever seen.

A baby is a summer rosebud
Petals folded snugly in
While waiting for love's liquid sun
To warm its tiny heart and let its
Natural flowering begin.

A baby is an autumn harvest
Gathered by an unseen hand
From chromosomes of half a million
Prior plantings old and distant
Newly sown in modern land.

A baby is a winter snowflake
Soft and frail in blankets white
Descending from the clouds of heaven
With a whisper for a warning
In the middle of the night.

Beginnings

Today is one of beginning for us:
    The dawn of an ice blue year
Made special by the welcome birth
    Of a tiny babe.
We start anew with you,
    Precious baby,
As you begin your journey through
    The years of mortality.
Your birth marks a change, a turn
    Of the road in our lives—
Home will never be the same as
    Yesterday for us.
Each new baby brings an
    Avalanche of love
As walls and hearts expand
    With joy to make room.

Beginnings are happy times:
    Days on which we look
Forward with hope, expectation
    And promise.
Sweet little child, may God help us
    In these days of newness
To weave the thread of your life
    Entrusted to our care
Into that great tapestry in such
    A way as pleases Him.
Then in that far day when these
    Beginnings are but faded memory,
We shall look at you and know the
    Joy of promises fulfilled.

My Query

How well did you know my mother,
    Little baby, newly born?
You have just come straight from Heaven
    On this cool October morn,
And my mother must have been there
    To kiss you and say farewell
When you left those Heavenly mansions
    And came to earth to dwell.

How well did you know my mother,
    Precious spirit from on high?
Did she ever tell you stories
    Or sing you a lullabye?
Did she ever hold you close to her
    As she did for me, a child,
And rock you gently in her arms
    And soothe you with her smile?

How well did you know my mother,
    Little baby soft and new?
While you were still in Heaven
    Did she teach and counsel you?
Did she tell you all about life here,
    Explain what you would see,
And share with you the many things
    She knows concerning me?

How well did my mother know you,
    Pretty baby, sweet and small?
Did she know what you would look like
    With your curly hair and all?
Did she know your personality
    So well that she could see
The kind of person you'd become
    And what your life would be?

How well did my mother know you
    In those lofty realms above,
As well as she knew me for years
    With sure, eternal love?
I often wish my mother could have
    Known you here on earth,
And yet I'm sure she knew you well
    Before your mortal birth.

Every Baby

Every baby has a face,
    But none looks just like you;
Every baby has two eyes,
    But yours are a special blue;
Every baby has two hands
    That clap and wave and cling;
Each baby voice is a melody,
    But a sweeter song you sing;
Most babies have a lock of hair,
    But none match your red curls;
All babies come as gifts from God
    And especially little girls.

First Son

September's last morn dawned
   bright and chill,
But his heart was ablaze with
   warmth and joy;
The world began for two
   that hour—
A new father and his
   first-born boy!

To A New Arrival

You were only three days old
   When first I saw your tiny face
And sleeping all oblivious
   To those who shyly sought a place
Outside the window where you lay.

My heart grew warm at sight of you:
   Unblemished, pure, and just as sweet
As blossoms from the hand of God.
   So recently you'd left His feet
You had a holy glow that day.

Your mother wore an angel's smile
   And pride was in your father's eyes,
Your brothers seemed to sense that you
   Had brought a change into their lives:
The family circle welcomed you.

Oh, precious baby, as you grow,
   Give heed to your dear father's voice,
And follow in your mother's steps
   That all who love you may rejoice,
And happiness crown all you do.

Perfect Pattern

He is six months old,
Robust, fair, and dimpled,
Molded in miniature
In the image of
His father.

As the man is twice reflected
In the small one's dark eyes mirror,
So are we all created
In the image of
Our God.

At Breakfast

A scrambled egg
A slice of toast
A couple strips of bacon
A glass of milk
And most of all
Two smiling little faces
That sit across the table
And with songs and spills
And laughter
Make breakfast time
A special part
Of all the hours we spend
Together.

Double Portion

Twice as many diapers,
   Twice as many pins,
Twice as many bottles
   When you're feeding twins;
Twice as many blankets,
   Twice as many bills,
Twice as many groceries,
   Twice as many spills;
Twice as many headaches,
   Twice as many chores,
Twice as many evenings
   Pacing on the floors;
Twice as many noises,
   Twice as many toys,
But there's no mistaking
   Twice as many joys;
Twice as many pleasures,
   Twice as many smiles,
Having twins makes living
   Doubly worth the trials;
Twice as many blessings
   And with twice the fun,
Life would be half empty
   If we had just one.

Surprise Package

We bought a layette the right size for one,
  We borrowed one strong wooden crib;
We picked out the name we like best of all
  And embroidered it onto a bib.

We thought we'd prepared for our baby to come,
  We waited with impatient grins;
But you may have guessed that we were the ones
  Who were blessed to be parents of twins.

Prayer for our Baby

Dear Lord, our baby's coming home.
She hadn't long to dwell with us on earth,
But in those few short hours she lived and breathed,
Our hearts were glad; we thanked Thee for her birth.
But now dear Lord, she's coming home to Thee
Where in Thy presence all her hours she'll spend,
And happiness eternal shall be hers
Because Thou art her Father and her friend.

Please let her know how truly she was wanted,
That we welcomed her arrival from above,
We longed to help her grow, protect and teach her,
And to share with her our home, our lives, our love.
Please help us, Lord, to set our lives in order
So that one day soon beyond this veil of tears,
We can meet again our precious little daughter
And dwell with her throughout the endless years.

Adopted Child

I knew, somehow,
at the first electric touch
of your little fingers
and mine
that I not only wanted you,
but you had chosen
me!
How could this be?
You came through other flesh
than mine,
your face was stamped with genes
from someone neither you nor I
would ever know.
But on that sun-glad morning
you, child, were given to me—
a blessed gift
out of my deepest longing.
Though I could not give you life,
yet you were mine
and we could share
the coming rainbow years
together.
The miracle fulfilled in us
I do not wholly understand,
but I am well content
as you are
knowing it was planned.

Perception

I walked today with my children three
In the quiet lane where I wished to be;
I left the dishes at home in the sink
For I needed space to breathe and think.

Three fragile voices sang delight
In a miniature waterfall, silvery-bright,
Exclaimed at leaves, falling one by one,
And praised the warmth of the autumn sun.

I walked today with my children three
And saw things my eyes alone could not see.

Published by courtesy of *The Relief Society Magazine*,
May 1969.

Friendship

To a little girl a friend is a small puppy
Who wags his tail and returns wet kisses
And doesn't bite;
And it is a grown up who holds her small hand
Firmly in his and whistles a tune as
They walk together.
A friend is someone else just her same size
Who shares cookies and doll clothes
And says with her eyes,
"I like you, too."

At Parting

Tenderly away in bed of white satin
You lay her, your first-born daughter,
Asleep in that solemn slumber
Imposed by the lullabye of angels.

Take one last look at her tiny face
And minute fingers, tightly curled;
Frame this picture with silver memories
To hang secure in a cherished spot
In a secret room of your heart.

Weep not on little dresses never worn
Nor over babbling words unspoken;
Grieve not for faltering footsteps
Never taken by your side;
The flowing years will see other hands
Clasped tight about your neck
And hear other springtime voices
Call you "Dad" and "Mom."

The Lord in Heaven is ever aware
Of each precious seed He plants in His Garden—
Your tiny sleeping rose-bud, too,
One day
Will have a time to bloom.

Too Soon Grown

Today I look upon my daughter
  Sleeping sweetly in her bed,
A precious treasure, small and dainty,
  Golden curls about her head,
With cheeks the hue of sun-kissed peaches,
  Open lips and four white teeth,
Two chubby arms stretched out above her
  Head to form a cherub wreath.

She's tiny now and so dependent
  On her mother's loving care,
If I could keep her this way always,
  Innocent and pure and fair,
How happy I would be! and yet
  I know her happiness depends
On growing, learning, and advancing,
  Serving God and making friends.

A tear escapes; too soon tomorrow
  Will be here and she'll be grown.
The days rush by, before I know it
  She'll have children of her own.
Dear Father, through these next short years
  Please help me guide her tender feet
In paths of happiness eternal;
  My teaching hours are few and fleet.

To Parents

Oh, come with me back to Babyland,
That "no,no," "mustn't touch," "maybe" land,
Where everything's tall
And you are so small—
That often bewildering Babyland.

Recall in your journey through Babyland
The heartache that follows a reprimand,
Remember your tears,
Your frustrations and fears,
When a dark shadow falls across Babyland.

Resolve that your little one's Babyland
Will be a secure, warm and happyland.
Take time out to play,
To be thoughtful and gay,
For one spends precious few years in Babyland.

Sometimes I Wonder

What would you do with a sly little elf
   Only thirty-one inches tall
If you woke up some morning to find seven eggs
   Scrambled all over the hall?

What would you do with Sir Mischief himself
   If you went in the bathroom and found
That he'd scrubbed out the tub and the floor and the rug
   With the cleanser and wasted a pound?

What would you do with a quick little scamp
   When he runs through the mud in new shoes?
And adds his own touch to your just-painted walls
   With the crayons—bright reds and bold blues?

What would you do with a vixen so small
   When the garbage is dumped on the floor
And the last seven pages torn out of that book
   You were reading?   But need I say more?

Sometimes I wonder if I can endure,
   I'm weary in body and brain;
But the sweet little imp is so dear to my heart
   That I smile—'till he does it again!

Growing Pains

When does a baby stop being a baby—
At seven or two or nineteen?
When do his parents consider him grown-up—
At some unpredictable age in-between?

Most likely his babyhood ceases abruptly
When new baby brother appears on the scene!

Baby's Toys

For baby's first birthday we bought some new toys:
A pull-along duck with a loud quacking noise,
A fish for the tub, and a brown fuzzy fox,
But the "gift" baby plays with the most is the box!

One More Day

I do not know the number of my days
nor if this crimson blaze on western hills
shall be my final glimpse
of earth-warming sun
but for this one more day
I thank thee, Lord.
For one more day to breathe sweet air
of Utah valleys, heavy
with perfume of new-cut hay,
For one more day to weed the row
of beans and corn, to help them grow
a little nearer to the harvest.
Thank thee, Lord, for one more day
to hold my child upon my knee,
for one more story softly read,
for time to kiss a tear and patch
the bruise upon his head.

And yet, dissatisfaction clouds my view
as I remember weaknesses and
goals unreached and tasks I did not do.

Please, Lord, grant me one more day
that I might try
to be more patient, that my
loving, kind example might be seen
by little watching eyes.
Give me one more day to walk the valley paths,
to smile
and send the echo of a cheerful song
across the rooftops of my world.

Give me one more evening hour to tuck
my little ones in bed, to kiss
each curly tousled head, to hear
each simple, pleading prayer.
Let me stand
for one more night beneath the stars
while through my hair
a breeze plays soft symphonic chords
and love holds tight my hand.

For one more day or, should it be
thy will, for days in multiplicity
I thank thee, Lord.